The Great Castle Fair

by Holly Harper

illustrated by Isabel Muñoz

OXFORD
UNIVERSITY PRESS
AUSTRALIA & NEW ZEALAND

Chapter 1
The castle ruins

Finn and his family were on a tour of a castle.

"The castle is in ruins now," said the guide, "but hundreds of years ago this was a crowded place full of excitement."

"Every year, the people in the castle would hold the Great Castle Fair," said the guide.

"There was a feast in the Great Hall and boys of your age worked as pages. The job of a page was to help with chores around the castle."

The guide pointed to the gardens. "There was also a jousting tournament here where brave knights competed to win," she said.

Finn closed his eyes and tried to imagine the Great Castle Fair. Life must have been very different back then!

When he opened his eyes again, he noticed a strange
green door. Finn was sure it hadn't been there a moment ago.
He walked over to it and opened it up a crack.

"There you are!" said a voice.

Chapter 2
The feast

There was a girl on the other side of the door.

"I've been looking for you, Page," she said. "Come with me."

Finn wasn't quite sure what was happening. The girl seemed to think he was a page in the castle. He followed the girl. He wanted to see what would happen next!

Finn followed the girl into the kitchen. A busy cook handed him a pie. It smelled delicious!

"There you are, Page!" said the cook. "Take that pie to the queen and be quick about it!"

Finn hurried out of the kitchen to the Great Hall.

He couldn't believe his eyes – it looked so different now.

There was a throne, a fireplace with a hearth and a

chandelier hanging from the ceiling.

"I must have gone back in time!" he gasped.

The queen sat on her throne at the table. Finn brought the pie over to her.

"Here's your pie, Your Majesty," he said.

"Thank you, Page," said the queen. "I have another job for you. Go and see what's bothering Sir Seymour."

Chapter 3
Sir Seymour

Finn noticed a knight in a suit of armour sitting at the table. He looked a bit flustered.

"What's wrong, Sir Seymour?" he asked.

Sir Seymour gave a loud sigh. "I'm supposed to compete in the jousting competition today. I've lost my lucky helmet. I don't think I can win without it!"

Just then, Finn heard a trumpet.

"Oh no!" said Sir Seymour. "The jousting competition is starting! What am I going to do?" He jumped up and ran out of the Great Hall towards the gardens.

Everybody started to leave the Great Hall and gather in the gardens. Finn followed them out. As he walked down the garden path, he noticed something under a bush. Could it be Sir Seymour's lucky helmet?

Chapter 4
The joust

Finn took the helmet and ran over to where Sir Seymour was getting ready for the joust. "Sir Seymour!" he called out. "Is this your helmet?" He threw it up to Sir Seymour.

"My lucky helmet!" Sir Seymour cried. He slipped it on.
"Thank you, Page. Now I can't lose."

The queen raised her hand for the joust to begin.

Sir Seymour lowered his lance and galloped at the rings.

Finn held his breath. He was worried for Sir Seymour.

He hoped he would win!

Chapter 5
The golden medal

"Sir Seymour is the winner!" announced the queen.
Everybody cheered and Finn joined in.

The queen held up a golden medal. "This is for you, Sir Seymour," she said.

Sir Seymour shook his head. "I couldn't have won without this page's help. I think you should give it to him instead."

The queen gave Finn the medal and the crowd began to cheer again.

"Good job, Page," she said.

"Thank you, Your Majesty," said Finn. Then he noticed the sun was starting to set. He realised he'd been gone all day. His mum and dad would be worried about him!

"Goodbye, Sir Seymour! Goodbye, Your Majesty!" he said. "I've had fun, but I've got to get back to my family in my own time!"

Finn waved and went back to the castle to find the strange green door.

Chapter 6
Back to normal

Everything was normal on the other side of the door. Finn caught up to the tour group just as it was leaving the Great Hall.

"Sorry, I've been gone all day," he said.

"Oh?" said his mum. "What are you talking about?"

"You were only gone for a minute," said his dad.

"What?" Finn asked, surprised. "But it felt like I was gone for so long!" He looked down and saw that the golden medal was missing.

'I must have imagined the whole thing,' Finn thought to himself. 'I guess I wasn't really at the Great Castle Fair after all.' Finn was confused. The adventure had seemed so real!

Finn followed his mum and dad out of the castle and into the garden.

"Here we have some statues of people who once lived in the castle," said the guide.

Finn looked up and saw that some of the statues looked *very* familiar.

"It's the queen," he gasped, "and Sir Seymour!"

The last statue was even more familiar and it had a medal around its neck.

Finn couldn't believe his eyes!